Suspicious eyes taints the heart

Elsie Violet

Ark House Press
arkhousepress.com

Cataloguing in Publication Data:
Title: Suspicious Eyes Taints the Heart
ISBN: 978-1-7636468-5-8 (pbk)
Subjects: Poetry; Prose;
Other Authors/Contributors: Violet, Elsie

Part illustrations designed by Quan Tre
Design by initiateagency.com

Acknowledgements

MY FAMILY
Firstly, I would like to acknowledge and give thanks, from the bottom of my heart to Daniel Asiata, Rhys Gunn, Isobel Joyner and Manaia Tither-Asiata, for their physical roles of love, grace, patience, and forgiveness in the tail-end years of writing this book. Love you all endlessly!

To my family in NZ, Australia, UK, U.S.A and Scotland – aunties, uncles, brothers, cousins, nieces, nephews, extended family, stepfamily, and in-laws – there is a little piece of all of you in this book, because a little of me was shaped by a little of you. Arohanui always.

Acknowledgements of the heart go out to: Grandma, Grandad, Rhys Hughes, Mason, Uncle Reya and Aunty Tina – gone but not forgotten! The impact you all had on my heart was great, and the memories will be forever.

MY FRIENDS
My girls and my church family!! Where would I be without you all! Although you are all scattered across NZ and Australia, you each hold a piece of my heart, and I am truly blessed to have been gifted and entrusted with your hearts too.
You all know who you are – thank you, and I love you.

ARKHOUSE PRESS
With a special shoutout to James! Thank you for taking a chance on me and for effortlessly guiding me through the unknown path of 'publishing'.

Contents

PART ONE
LITTLE GIRL LOST

A dark and morbid time for me - where I struggled to find myself and where I fit in this world. It was a very lonely time in my life. Every day felt like a war. It was me against the world …

A loving mum – a caring dad,
These are things I never had.
My mother was always cruel and unfair,
My father is a stranger – he was never there!

No family life for me to enjoy,
Alone in the world – the neglected tomboy.
Yelled at and beaten – left broken on the floor,
Nothing could save me – not even the law!

Little girl lost with no-where to go,
Trapped in that prison – covering bruises like a pro.
No one aware of the war that raged within me,
Everything bottled up – I didn't let anyone see!

With no love, no friends, and no self-esteem,
I yearned for an escape – death was my dream.
Failed attempts left me angrier at the world,
What more could go wrong for this lost little girl?!

COULD IT BE POSSIBLE?

I've always wondered, is there really a hell?
Could it be possible for it to exist so well?

Do you have to die to meet the devil?
Could it be possible that I have already met the rebel?

Once you're in hell – can you escape the burning fires?
Could it be possible that the angels have been liars?

My life so far has been my hell,
I've been locked up in an invisible cell.

I hope in the future I find the courage in me,
To escape these burning fires – to finally be free!

WHO AM I??

Who am I? What am I like?
Am I a black person or am I white?
Who are my enemies? Who are my friends?
Am I a loner just filled with dead ends?
What makes me laugh? What makes me cry?
Do I give up easily or do I try and try?
What makes me live? Why shouldn't I die?
Should I end my life now or continue living a lie?

CONFUSED

It's really hard being like me,
Trying to hide away from reality.
What am I running from – why do I hide?
Why do I feel so empty deep down inside?
How can I lead an ideal life?
One without drama – one without strife?
There doesn't seem to be a ready solution…
So I'll just have to stay amidst my own confusion!

DEPRESSED

I am staring at the big world outside,
Staying under-covers – trying to hide.
Running away from all the unruly fights,
Keeping to myself because reality bites.
Afraid of revealing too much of myself,
Never asking for any-one's un-necessary help.
Alone in the world – separated from the rest,
I have my own little corner – my own little nest.
I have no one to run to when I am happy inside,
I have no one to cry on when I want to lay down and die.
Troubles and worries are pushed deep down inside,
Control yourself girly – you are not allowed to cry!

BAD FEELINGS

Sometimes thoughts of suicide enter my head,
I say to myself that I would be better off dead.
I've pondered many times on how I could end it all,
But everything scares me and my time I stall.
I can't handle the thought of self-inflicting pain,
It would be so much easier if there was someone else to blame.
So God if you're listening and you want to make me happy,
Please take my life now and make it snappy!

A TRUE FRIEND

Tears are always on the brink of explosion,
A true friend in your life? What a crazy notion!
No one cares what you do or where you are,
You are alone in this world – you are just a blah!
Blah means nothing of importance – just a being,
No life, no love and no one seeing!
No one seeing your pain or your unspoken needs,
No one seeing the extent of how your heart bleeds!
Well now it's time to take a stand…
Just come with me – here take my hand…
Say goodbye to this world and take a bow…
Don't be afraid – I'm here with you now…
I'll stay with you right to the end,
I am your angel of death – your only true friend!

TANGAROA

I'm sitting on the sands of the beach of Browns Bay,
The waves are coming for me – they want me to play,
They're coming closer and closer to take me away,
Perhaps in the water I will stray…

Tangaroa has come for me – he won't let go,
He's pulling me and pulling me way down below,
I'm begging for my life – all I hear is 'NO',
My only choice is to slowly let go…

I'm going under – it's getting so deep,
I'm opening my eyes – I just want to peep,
I see the beautiful children of my life taker and weep,
I'm closing my eyes now – I'm in a deep sleep!

A LIFE IS SLIPPING AWAY

The girl has tears all down her face,
The air is filled with her screaming.
She doesn't hear her heartbeat race,
As she watches him fall from the ceiling.

...a life is slipping away.

Her feet are running faster and faster,
Bringing her closer to his body,
She watches him shake and sees the disaster,
The ground by his head is bloody.

...a life is slipping away.

A crowd has gathered out of no-where,
Everyone just standing and staring.
They are all paralysed with their shared fear,
Will his death be near?

...a life is slipping away.

The ambulance has come but it's too late,
For his being has become an empty pod.
A bittersweet encounter as she ponders his fate,
And she whispers to herself 'why not me God?'

...a life has slipped away.

PART TWO
STRENGTH OF A WOMAN

I have discovered the strength within me that can take me to places that I never imagined before. My heart has become lighter and less filled with hate ....

Reading those poems – feeling my pain,
Has made me realize how much I have truly changed.
That used to be me – writing about my hate for the world,
How could so much anger be locked inside that little girl?

My friends attempted to lure me out of that shell,
They showed me there was happiness outside of my hell.
They became a light in the darkness that filled my world,
With them by my side I farewelled that little girl!

So here I am now – all grown up and mature,
No more death in my heart – no more pain to endure.
I have let go of my past – no longer does it enslave me,
With new hope in my heart – I am finally free!

CHAT GROUP BUDDEEZ!

So much has happened in so little time,
And with each scenario I created a rhyme!
Lyrical storms raged within my mind,
Poetry was the only outlet I could find.

This lyrical storm is raging inside me again,
Words flowing too fast to be written by pen.
My inspiration this time is the support of my peers,
My soul-sista friends who have calmed all my fears!

Their cheerful words and songs of praise,
That is what got me through those awful days.
They were my strength when I couldn't go on,
Thanks to their support – those awful days are gone!

LADYLUVS

You give me strength when I don't want to go on,
You give me hope when I feel all the light has gone.
You push me when I float in no direction,
You give me an answer before I've even asked the question.
You understand my madness when I'm amidst my despairs,
You give me comfort when I think no one else cares.
You tell me I'm wrong when I've been naughty in the night,
You tell me I'm beautiful when I know I'm a fright.
You've been there for me whenever I've reached out for you,
And I pledge to the end that I'll be there for you too!

FREE TO BE ME

I won't conform to the norm of what others think I should be
With my poker-face on – I choose what the world sees of me.
No fear, no tears – no emotions for you to see
I will fight to be free – I will fight to be me!

DREAMER

I dream of a life as simple as can be,
No matters to solve – it's problem free.
No wars to fight – no wounds to heal,
No material things for us to steal.

I dream of a love so tender and true,
No bad words – just I love you.
No broken hearts and no divorce,
No living in a marriage with total remorse.

I dream of things I know I can't get,
Because the genie I haven't yet met.
With my eyes wide shut – a dreamer I am,
I will always dream – just because I can!

ME MYSELF & I

I find it hard to say how I feel,
Everything builds up and starts to congeal!
I'm afraid of what others might think or say,
So I deal with things in a different way!

I write down things I could never say out loud,
Things that could cause a thunderous cloud!
Things that are bad and I might regret,
Things that are sad and I'd rather forget!

Poetry is my creative way of expression,
If I didn't have that I would turn to aggression!
I'm not trying to say that I'm a great poet,
I just start off a sentence and then I flow it!

LYRICAL STORM!

Words, rhymes, verses, and form,
I can't stop what's inside me – a lyrical storm!
Life, feelings, experiences and more,
All creating a fire within me – poetry galore!
Release, calmness, growth, and freedom,
Nothing holding me back – my imagination is my kingdom!

POETRY FOR ME

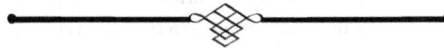

When I'm feeling lost and in disarray
Poetry puts into words what my heart cannot say
Writing is my release, my force – my unrequited passion
Not a hobby, a trend, or a passing fashion
It's a feeling, a being – a series of moments in my life
I need it, I want it – my comfort when in strife

ANGEL

Here I am – your angel in disguise,
Aiming to please – hoping to surprise.
My halo is faintly seen in the heavenly skies,
My wings are all around you – my butterflies!

I will give you my halo to soothe your sighs,
I will give you my angel dust to ease your cries.
I will give you my wings to shelter you from the lies,
I will give you my all before your belief truly dies!

With nothing left of me to give – I will await my demise,
By giving you my soul – I will open your eyes.
I will show you that angels are real – although the world still denies,
We are all around you – the enchanted butterflies!

LOVE

Love is a word that is so easily spoken,
Over-rated in it's glory – a promise so easily broken.
Versatile in its form and so often misunderstood,
Ever-changing in it's sensation – so bad and yet so good!

BOYS WILL BE BOYS

Boys will be boys – it's the way of life,
Confusing the girls and causing us strife.
Unaware of the chaos they leave behind,
'Ignorance is bliss' – this cliché defined!

Girls will be girls – this is also the way,
Analysing the boys and hoping everything is ok.
Unaware of the chaos we leave behind,
Hoping true love we will one day find!

Boys and girls somehow joining together,
Believing their partnership will last forever.
But girls will be girls and boys will be boys,
Nothing lasts forever …but we'll remember the joys!

TRUE LOVE

Everybody laughing – everybody drinking,
A beautiful boy across the room seductively winking.
Everybody dancing – everybody moving,
Him and I on the dance floor intimately grooving.
Everybody leaving – my friends are leaving too,
Him and I caught up in the flirtation without even a clue.
Everybody hustling, hurrying off home,
Him and I at the taxi stand – I am going home alone!
You see…true love is the man who comes to me sober,
With a love that doesn't expire when the night is suddenly over

LATEST CRUSH

Thoughts of my crush causing crazy desire,
Memories of our closeness turning my hormones on fire.
His image, his interests – makes me want to learn more,
His smile, his playfulness – causes tremors to my core.
His jokes, his sarcasm – gives me the giggles inside,
His friendship, his closeness – meant in him I could confide.
These thoughts and feelings I must never show,
These feelings are not mutual so they can never grow!

SWEET SUGAR CANDY LIPS

Sweet sugar candy lips – connecting with mine,
Sweet sugar candy lips – feeling so divine.
Sweet sugar candy lips – tasting like wine,
Sweet sugar candy lips – won't you be mine!

RETURN TO SENDER

Your touch does things to me I can't explain,
Where-ever you touch me – I feel some sort of pain!
This pain does not harm me – it does not tear me apart,
This pain must be because you are holding my heart!

I love you so much it hurts inside,
It would crush me all over if I found out you lied!
Please be careful with my heart – be very tender,
Don't ever send it back saying 'return to sender'!

FUN AND GAMES

Fun and games – a concept so new to me,
Sex without love – how can this be?
Erotic moments stolen when we're together,
No feelings at stake – just pure pleasure.

Fun and games – I want to play,
No strings attached in any way.
Just two friends playing safely together,
Both of us aware that this won't last forever.

Fun and games – will you play with me?
Naughty friends in the night we will be.
Nothing will change – our friendship will last,
Let's play this game and have a blast!

FUN AND GAMES – PART II

Fun and games – a concept so tempting to me,
But sex without love does not come for free.
Friendships destroyed and self-respect is lost,
All this and more – is it worth the cost?

Fun and games – I don't want to play anymore,
I'd rather be alone than be labelled a whore.
Friendships are saved and my self-respect is kept,
Under the reality carpet this notion is swept!

SERENDIPITY

If I tumble, will you break my fall?
If I'm lost, will you hear my call?
If I cry, will you wipe my tears?
If I am scared, will you calm my fears?

No words of I-told-you-so to be said ...
No words of judgment to fill my head ...
No words of anger to make me see red ...
No words of what I should have done instead ...

If I'm tired, will you hear my yawn?
If I'm cold, will you keep me warm?
If I'm troubled, will you make things bright?
If I succeed in life, will you share my light?

No thoughts of the past to hold you back ...
No thoughts of anger to get you off track ...
No thoughts of 'what-if' to cloud the facts ...
No thoughts of insecurity to cause the cracks ...

I pledge to give you all the above,
The good and the bad – it's all part of our love.
Forget about the notion of sense and sensibility,
Together we can create our own serendipity!

WHAT-IF

Rumour mill speeding down the highway of life,
Only myself to blame for this moment of strife!
Secret words whispered in my drunken state of mind,
The secrecy of my crush completely undermined!

Can't stop thinking of the way he makes my heart melt,
Yet afraid of what could happen if he knew how I felt!
So many reasons to hide how I'm feeling inside,
Too scared to approach him and swallow my pride!

These feelings so raw and all over the place,
Can't control the tears that run down my face!
Thoughts of 'what if' always running thru my mind,
This sunken feeling in my heart is depression defined!

On the outside I show my perfect work of art,
A fake smile on my face and a brand-new start.
No more thinking of what was or what could be,
Secret feelings of my crush has become history!

Nothing will ever happen – I can finally see,
We were meant to be friends and that's all we'll ever be!
It's time to move on and enjoy the friend I have in him,
Live up the single life and stop being so grim!

So sad inside for things I must hide,
No one to confide about how my heart lied,
Tears have dried from the waterfalls I've cried,
No more feelings inside …has my soul died?

CLOUD 9

Lose my thoughts in a cloud of smoke,
Don't need much – just one toke.
Inhale, exhale – fogging my mind.
Inner peace I want to find!

Tears are clearing…
A smile is appearing…
Abyss bliss is nearing…
No more caring!

High as a kite – so alive and free,
No more tears trying to escape me.
No more pain in my heart to make me cry,
No more questions of why, why, why!!!

Giggles escape me…
The fog has saved me…
Dreamless sleep shades me…
Reality evades me!

COUNTERFEIT LOVE

Counterfeit love causing sparks of desire,
Hormones ablaze with a lustful fire.
Naughty thoughts playing havoc with our mind,
Controlled by our urges   sensibility is left behind.

Counterfeit love causing crazy notions,
Filling our minds with fantasy love potions.
Aware of the game and its many rules,
Yet unable to stop ourselves from playing the fools.

Counterfeit love causing fear in our hearts,
Lust or Love – how can we tell them apart?
Our head says one thing, but heart does not obey,
Nothing there to save us when counterfeit love gets our way!

SEA OF TEARS

Hurting, hurting deep down inside,
A sea of tears I have cried.
Two hearts beating – one heart lied,
One friend down – the friendship died!

Tears for him – tears for me,
Tears for what can never be.
Tears for what my heart did not see,
Tears for memories that were me and T.

Weeping, weeping – I'm all cried out,
No-where to turn except inside out.
No one to understand my saddened pout,
Nothing within and everything without!

Tears for things not undone,
Tears for he who was the one.
Tears for wishing I had a gun,
Tears for my heart – constantly on the run!

GOODBYE

Too tired to think yet too scared to close my eyes,
Because you will appear and inside my heart cries.
Too many memories yet so many lies,
A friendship left in limbo – there were no goodbyes.

Too afraid to let go of something I held so dear,
A bond I thought would last forever – nothing could compare.
Too proud to call you and ask if you have a minute to spare,
I'm not part of your life now – you've made that quite clear.

Too much energy wasted on memories of what used to be,
Always there for each other – that was you and me,
Too afraid to close the door on us – but it must be done I now see,
In this poem I say goodbye – I'm setting my heart free.

THE END

It's finally over – it was doomed from the start,
Although I had doubts – I still gave him my heart!
Now the questions can end – about us, about my-self,
I can focus on the future as I nurse my heart back to health!

It's time to let go and move on with my life,
No more baggage to carry that was my relationship strife!
The tear drops are proof of the pain in my heart,
But these tears also mark the day of my brand-new start!

VICIOUS CYCLE

Screaming, screaming in my head,
Vision blurring – seeing red.
Wishing you gone – wishing you dead,
Envisioning my fist connecting with your head.

But nothing happens – it all stays the same,
Some words escape me, but my actions remain tame.
Bad words exchanged – hurting each other is the aim,
Both standing our ground – refusing to take the blame.

Sadness weighing heavy in my heart,
A love-less union right from the start.
Comfort we sought – 'fun' was our art,
A baby was born and tore all that apart.

Now priorities have changed and here I stay,
A father for my child and help keeping the bills at bay.
This vicious cycle repeated day after day,
The screaming, the sadness – is there no other way?

DEAR DIARY

As I lay on my bed staring at the ceiling,
I ask myself why I feel what I'm feeling.
There's pain in my heart causing these tears,
Pain caused by men who have embedded these fears.
Fears of me enjoying a man's loving touch,
Fears of me perhaps loving someone else too much.
I can't let myself feel too deep too fast,
As experience tells me that love never lasts.
I must keep my feelings well hidden from the world,
Because dear diary – I'm just a girl

CRAZY PHASE

So many things lurking in my mind…
A quick escape I need to find…
My exterior strength is undermined…
Lala fog creates my comfy cloud nine!

Friends are worried about this phase…
Aware this might not be a passing craze…
Concerned for my need of the lala haze…
Afraid of how this will affect my mental maze!

Fear not my friends I'll be alright…
My goals in life are still in sight…
My friends and family will see me right…
My children are my force – my will to fight!

SO MIXED UP

Feeling sad – feeling blue,
So empty inside without even a clue!
Tears emerging at the corner of my eye,
I'm crying again but I don't know why!

Frustrations gnawing from the inside out,
Fear of the unknown and my own self-doubt!
Nothing to calm this whirlwind of emptiness,
Stuck in this depression of utter loneliness.

Surrounded by loved ones yet still alone,
Fighting inner battles – exploring the unknown!
So sad for what was and what can never be,
No one else out there seems to love me for me!

Parental responsibilities keeping me grounded in life,
The love for my children keeping me out of strife.
Resisting the urge to get lost in the lala haze,
Facing my demons in life's never-ending maze!

BABY IT'S YOU (song)

Your almond eyes and straight black hair,
Your inquisitive nature and lack of fear.
Your quick little temper and crocodile tears,
Your naughty words and evil stares!

The reason I smile thru my tears...
The reason I stand and face my fears...
The reason I fight my inner taboos...
Oooooooh...baby it's you!

Your beautiful voice as your sing your songs,
Your lovable hugs that right all your wrongs.
Your independent stance that makes you strong,
Your grunting snores that last all night long...!

The reason I smile thru my tears...
The reason I stand and face my fears...
The reason I fight my inner taboos...
Oooooooh...baby it's you!

Your unconditional love brings out the best in me,
Your tender innocence ignites the hope within me.
You're my heart, my soul – my everything to me,
It is YOU dear Rhys that truly completes me!

The reason I smile thru my tears...
The reason I stand and face my fears...
The reason I fight my inner taboos...
Oooooooh...baby it's you!

I WILL SURVIVE

Who would sit all day and contemplate the big C?
Until this day, I never thought it would be me!
But here I am on day number four,
Struggling thru my workload – constantly looking at the door!

Thinking about things that could have been,
Opening my eyes to things I should have seen.
Crying on the inside for what can never be,
Wondering what the morbid future holds for me.

A loving relationship with Rhys' father is unseen,
A caring mother for my brother is still a dream.
An age-stopping device for my grandma is not even in existence,
And now the big C has entered my life with great persistence.

What more could go wrong – what else will life throw my way,
With so much negativity in my life – why would I want to stay?
The love for my son and my brother is the only thing keeping me alive,
With them in my life – the only option is to survive!

THESE CRYING EYES

Seven months have gone by – my how time flies,
It seems like only yesterday when I said my final goodbyes.

You were my lifesaver in childhood, but I was too young to realize,
Your love is what empowered me – you were my angel in disguise.

You were so full of memories Grandma – your words were so wise,
I took your company for granted Grandma – I failed to hear your cries.

I am brought to tears as your birthday nears – so aware of your untimely demise,
I wish you were here to stop these tears that keep falling from these crying eyes!

TWILIGHT TEARS

Alone with my thoughts as dawn draws near,
Silence singing out my pain and stirring my fear.
Gentle snores beside me add rhythm to the burden my heart bears,
An orchestra of loneliness surrounds me as I shed my twilight tears!

AFRAID TO HOPE

Quakes of fear trembling inside,
As poetry leaves my heart open wide!
Open for everyone to finally see,
That the bubbly exterior is not really me!

Afraid of the reactions my words will create …
Afraid of the friendships my words could deflate …
Afraid of the judgments my words will receive …
Afraid of the truth … will anyone believe?

A glimmer of hope within my heart,
As poetry explains my life of art!
The art of escaping my harsh reality,
Glazing the truth with life's formality!

Hoping my words will eject demons of my past …
Hoping my words will shed this bubbly mask …
Hoping my words will explain my inner confusion …
Hoping my words will create a happy conclusion!

EXERCISE TO EXORCISE

Salty sweat beads dripping carelessly into my eyes,
Washing out my worries – blinding me from life's lies!
Too exhausted to ponder what was and what will never be,
Mind is vacant, relaxed and completely stress free!

Pushing thru the pain - exorcising demons of yesterday,
Putting hope in my heart for a brighter today!
This is my release, my growth, my healing of the soul,
This keeps me alive, keeps me sane and keeps my heart whole!

MOURNING IN THE MORNING

5k's nonstop – pushing thru the pain,
I CAN do more, WILL do more – keep running in the rain!
Sore legs, sore heart – it's all the same,
As my sweat meets my tears in this tug of war game!

I will stay up, stay strong – keep going with life,
I am a woman, a mother but no longer a wife!
No more tears, no more fears – no more reason to mourn,
His actions, his loss – means my brand-new dawn!

I AM ONLY HUMAN

Being a fulltime working mother is not easy,
And it certainly wasn't my chosen path for me.
But here I am about to become a divorcee,
A new burden to bear as a broken family.

Feeling shunned by the world for his decisions in life,
Kicking me while I'm down and further twisting the knife.
Alone I stand with my kids while judgments run rife,
Nothing to cushion this relentless feeling of strife.

To the world I project that I stand tall and strong,
I carry on with life like as if nothing is wrong.
Isolated within my thoughts is where my troubles belong,
Allowing no one to see how weak I have been all along.

You may not have seen me cry while I was healing,
But that does not mean my heart bore no feeling.
To rock bottom I fell – all broken and bleeding,
While my smile masked the hurt of my heart grieving.

So know me before you judge me based on what you see,
And understand that there are always two sides to a story.
I may not cry out my pain in search of public sympathy,
But I am only human with the same need for a little empathy!

PART THREE
POETRY BECOMES MY TESTIMONY

In my previous poems, you will see how I cried out to God and questioned his existence. I even asked him to take my life many times. I think in this next chapter, you will be rather surprised about which direction life has taken me

I've always thought my poems were my testimony,
My life, my story - my words without harmony.
I wanted to help others who felt alone like me,
But today I was hit with an almighty epiphany…

…How can it be a testimony if there is no glory to God?

I am where I am through choices made along the way,
But who guided those steps each and every day?
Who kept the hope in my heart when I begged to be taken away?
Who placed Danny in my life when I kept the world at bay?
Many times I questioned Gods' place in my life,
If He loved me so much why would he give me such strife?
Escapism was my dream through the blade of a knife,
Many times I tried to end the sorry existence of my life.
But here I am today - stronger than ever before,
The heartache and pain is not my focus anymore.
Through all my struggles Gods strength came to the fore,
I just had to CHOOSE to walk through His open door.
With my eyes wide open and the truth in my heart,
My mind has been transformed - the old me torn apart.
Ploughing my field straight while aware of the fiery dart,
Thankful for His grace as I embrace my new start.
Thank you God for always leading the way,
For not taking my life when I begged you to every day.
Thank you for the purpose in my heart born from the pain of yesterday,
And thank you for the struggles that created the strength in me today.

JUST FRIENDS

For so long I lived so broken,
My pain always left unspoken,
My heart became a devils token,
My true essence was never awoken.

Now here I stand so tall and proud,
My true self no longer unavowed,
My core values are finally allowed,
My faith in God I shall sing out loud!

For He enabled me to love again,
He healed my hate towards all men,
He showed me life thru a poetic pen,
He gave me Danny as 'Just a friend'!

DANNYBOYS GIRL

Imperfect beings,
In this imperfect world,
Nothing feels more freeing,
Than being Danny-Boys girl.
For forever and a day,
I will give him my life,
That's the promise I made,
When he made me his wife.
In sickness and in health,
'Til death do us part,
Our love is our wealth,
As we hold each other's heart.

SAY A LITTLE PRAYER

A prayer a day,
Keeps the fiery darts away.
Nothing keeps the Holy Spirit stirred,
Like leaning into His almighty word!

IS THAT YOU LORD?

I feel a new drive within me,
Pushing me forward…
Is this the Holy Spirit in me?
Is that you in me Lord?
I feel empowered as a writer,
With your word as my sword…
Showing that even though I'm a fighter,
It is through YOU that I have been restored.
I feel renewed with your confidence,
As your light in me is poured…
Too many times to be labelled a coincidence,
Your presence can no longer be ignored.

NEW DIRECTION

I have put pen to paper my whole life,
But never have words been so rife.
They're tumbling out faster than I can write,
This new direction is going at the speed of light.
Jotting down words when and where I can,
No time to make sense of my scribbling hand.
This fire in my belly has me all ablaze,
His spiritual gift will no longer laze.
It's woken me up with a purpose inside,
It's full steam ahead on this wild ride.

REASON, SEASON, LIFETIME

I am who I am today, because of who I was yesterday.
I am standing right here, because of where I was yesteryear.
Everything happens for a reason, Gods' plan is our season.
Through the tough times He gave me, He led me to His eternity.
Forever thankful for His light, which led me through each dark night.
He was always there, but I just thought He didn't care.
Many times I cried out to die, because I thought His love for me was a lie.
But He was inside of me all along, keeping me alive and standing strong.
Reflecting now from the inside out, I can see how His plan has played out.
Too many times to be a coincidence, His presence is now my confidence.

WHY?

New Spiritual eyes,
My former self dies.
The past so full of lies,
And yet my soul still cries...
WHY?

Thankful for my life today,
Lessons learnt from yesterday.
Aware of my blessings every day
And yet my lips still struggle to pray...
WHY?

I called out for Him once before,
Lying broken and bitter on the floor.
Did not want to be saved anymore,
Death was all I wanted to implore.
And yet here I still am...
WHY?

How am I still here?
Through violence, escapism, illnesses, and fear...
All that and more has led me right here,
Is this why he didn't answer me yesteryear?

EVERYTHING HAPPENS FOR A REASON

The silence of night I used to always fear,
Because the sound of my thoughts I couldn't bear.
Negativity in my life left my mind in despair,
Insomnia ruled the night as I watched dawn draw near.

Loneliness and hurt haunted me every day,
A pitiful mess I became in every way.
Life lessons beat me down to my final fray,
T'was a daily struggle to keep the madness at bay.

But here I lay comfortably enveloped by night,
Strengthened by the wisdom of lessons in hindsight.
No more tears or fears preparing to take flight,
I feel strong as I stride proudly into Gods light!

Happy, healthy and at peace with my life,
I have finally let go of all my past strife.
Gone is the burden of negativity running rife,
I am a child of God first – then a mother and a wife!

HOME IS WHERE THE HEART IS

So content I am in this place called 'home',
No desire to wander, explore or roam.
My feet firmly planted in the ground,
No longer a need to move us around.
Foundations taken root where I stand,
Even though this place is a foreign land.
Home is where the heart is - this I see,
No-where else in the world I'd rather be.
Material things mean nothing to me,
My home will always be with my family.

SIT STAY AND PRAY

Raise your hands towards heavenly lands,
Seek His love by reaching above.
Call out His name and ignite your flame,
Let His fire burn and receive all that you yearn.

LET HIM IN

Take heed!
Your need to feed shall sow your seed.
He'll be your steed in lightning speed - your heart will be freed.
Just take the lead.

Don't be afraid - these plans He made were carefully laid.
Your debt repaid - the unjust trade.

No need to fear - let Him near - Let him hear your quiet prayer.

SICK BUT STRONG

I've been sick in my head, my heart, and my soul,
Even my body gave out and I was gone as a whole.
Bedridden and blue - unable to move,
A pit of despair with nothing left to lose.
Every morning I prayed for God to guide my way,
To help me live according to His word every day.
To heal me from these illnesses that stole my time,
To place forgiveness in my heart and free my mind.
Now here I stand much stronger than before,
Peace in place of where there was once war.
My faith was questioned out of deep-seated fear,
Little did I know of the true power of prayer.
My body still fails me, but my heart has been healed,
Because in His love, my future has been sealed.
This sickly vessel of mine still has much fruit to bear,
Poetry as my testimony will be all that's left for you to hear.

DAILY ARMOUR

Every day I wear the armour of God,
Because I _need_ Him to shield my sickly pod.
Fiery darts come from every direction,
And I _need_ His grace as daily protection.
His word convicts me every day,
I _need_ his guidance in every way.

I fail daily – this I know,
But I _need_ His strength to help me grow.
Every morning I seek Him out,
Because prayer-life washes away my doubt.
In God I find all that I need,
In His love – my heart is freed.

BELT OF TRUTH

Be a hearer and a doer...
Let your actions be the lure.
If you do what you say and say what you do...
Nothing in your life can ring as untrue.
Practice what you preach...
Live by what you teach.
If you say you're going to do it...
Make sure you follow through it.
Nothing worse than promises unkept...
Because empty words will show your true depth.
Don't be that person who is ok with living a lie...
Let Gods truth in your life ring long after you die.

STAY UP – PRAY UP!

When hope runs dry,
When life feels like a lie,
When you ask the world 'WHY?',
Cast your eyes to the sky!

When you feel your heart cry,
When your soul starts to die,
When you feel the end is nigh,
Raise your hands up high!

Let Him hear your cry,
It's never too late to try,
He will never ask why,
His love is not a lie,
The devil's foothold you must deny!

WAITING...

Eyes wide open, but I can't see...
Can't seem to focus on what's in front of me.
Blinded by heartache deep within me...
Afraid of what the future holds - feeling lost at sea.
Where to now? What is it that I can't see?
How many tears must I cry? When will His peace set me free?

SADNESS PRAYER

Tears on the brink as my heart sinks,
That broken link hurts more than you think.
Sadness is taking over me, fiery darts are wounding me,
Dear Lord please can you help me? I need your strength to set me free!
Please lead the way, guide my steps today,
Keep those thoughts at bay - In your name I pray...
Amen.

COMFORT PRAYER

Dear Lord, please hear my prayer,
As I seek you out to draw you near.
I need your guidance to show me the way,
I need your love to pave my way.

I need your wisdom inside my heart,
To show forgiveness against my fiery dart.
I need your comfort as I crumble inside,
These tears and fears please push aside.

I need so much, this I know,
Amidst despair there's no-where else I'd go.
So please dear Lord, hear my prayer,
Please touch my heart to show you're near.

THANK-YOU PRAYER

Thank you Lord for yet another day,
Another opportunity for me to pray.
Thank you for all the blessings in my life,
The love, the laughter, and even the strife.
For the strife led me to where I am now,
In Your house, in Your name, my head I bow.
Thank you for saving me from myself,
Even though I had rejected everyone else's help.
Thank you for being the best part of me,
Thank you for setting my heart free.

SPIRITUAL GIFT

His word thru mine,
This gift divine,
For you to see,
His truth in me!
Testing times,
Created rhymes,
A story to tell,
His love to spell!
Struggle and pain,
Not in vain,
My truth in Him,
His strength within!
Can you see...
Will you see...
What could be...
If you LET it be!

POETRYNMOTION

PoetryNmotion…
Shows my life in slow motion.
Where happiness is no longer just a notion,
And true love was found amidst the commotion.
With happiness in my mind, body, and soul,
Gods love in my heart has made me feel whole.
'True love and happiness' was always my goal,
This was not found until I gave up all sense of control.
#letgoandletGOD

RENEWAL OF MY MIND

Who loves to hate?
Eager to retaliate,
Quick to terminate,
No time to contemplate.

Throwing blame,
Inflicting pain,
Ego aflame,
A vicious game.

That used to be me!
Words at the ready,
Fighting for you to see,
Fighting for me to be free.

Everything was a fight!
In my darkest night,
I fell into my plight,
I lost my sight.

But NOW I see!
HE fights for me!
HE sees me!
HE has freed me!
no one else matters

No longer fighting to have my say
No more battling through my day
My mind renewed to see His way
And in His name I daily pray

ROMANS 12:2
Do not be conformed to this world, but be transformed by the renewal of your mind, that by
testing you may discern what is the will of God, what is good and acceptable and perfect.

GET FED

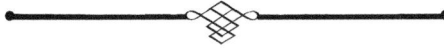

Let His word
Be your daily bread.
Let His truth
Keep you spiritually fed.
Let His sacrifice
Make your heart humble.
Let His guidance
Lift you up when you stumble.
Let God in your life
When you are overcome by fear.
Let Him calm your troubles

By connecting through prayer.

LOVE IS THE CURE

Leave room in your heart for forgiveness to grow,
Plough your field straight then reap what you sow.
Let love rule your actions through your mind and your heart,
Let God guide your steps to put you on the right path.
GIVE love and BE love with all that you say and do,
And always remember the love He showed when He laid on the cross for you.

PART FOUR
BEHIND THE MASK – BELOW THE SCARS

Oh how life changes when our faith becomes less about what God can do for us,
and more about what we can do for others in HIS strength, love and power....

A LITTLE ABOUT ME

My first childhood memory is when I was five years old - I explored the F word in front of my mother ... the consequences of that was a backhand across my face that threw me backwards with a force so great that it made me lose a tooth.

In my younger years, I was beaten with open-handed slaps, closed-fist punches, cricket bats, shoes, vacuum pipe hoses, tree branches, jug cords etc ... basically anything she could lay her hands on. If I cried during a beating, I would get another beating for crying. If someone tried to stop her from beating me, she would beat me again in front of them, to prove that she was in control, and they could not save me.

At age 11, the school principal called the Social Welfare Dept because I had gone to school with bruises up and down my arms and legs from a cricket bat beating, which was hidden with long pants and a long shirt. My PE teacher would not allow the class to start until we were all in correct clothes for the sport, and I was forced to take off my jumper, which revealed the bruises. Social Welfare came to the house and looked me over, then had a closed-door conversation with my mother. I remember that day so vividly because I thought they were going to save me from the hell I was living in ... but they did not! They just left me there! I do not know what she told them, but after that day, I lost all hope in the justice system, and in God.

As I grew from a child into a teenager, I learnt that apologies were laced with blame, and it was not her fault that she beat me, it was mine: 'I'm sorry I hurt you last night, but you know what I'm like when I'm drunk, you should have just stayed out of my way'. I learnt that any apology that starts with 'I'm sorry but...' is not an apology at all, just another way to tell me that I did something wrong to deserve the beating.

Between the ages of 12 & 16, I had attempted suicide multiple times, but always failed because I either did not swallow enough pills, or did not cut deep enough, or just hesitated too long at the last minute. I would run the streets late at night while she was passed out drunk, hoping that someone would kill me, because I could not kill myself ... but no, I always made it home safely somehow.

I doubted Gods very existence, and turned my heart against Him because if He 'loved me', why would He put me in that situation, AND, why wouldn't He take my life and save me from my miserable existence???

At age 15, I ran away from home and made the city streets of Auckland my home. I was a 'street-kid' and stereotyped as 'homeless' even though I had a home – and by age 16, I was working and studying part-time and staying with friends – never again to call that place I grew up in 'home'.

From these experiences and more as I grew from adolescence into adulthood, I became fiercely independent, and I protected my independence fiercely. I did not need anyone's help, and even if I did, I would not admit it, because that would be weak – and there was no room in my life for weakness!

As an adult, I have been in two physically violent/abusive relationships as well as other emotionally and verbally abusive relationships, and I have fled a country from the hands of an abusive partner when my child's life became threatened. To the untrained eye, it seemed that I could not escape the violence of other peoples' hearts, and I lost all hope in this thing called 'love'.

Now, in my later years of life, I have discovered something new ... MYSELF! My voice, my truth, and my desires. With the help of counselling, support groups, my church family, and my closest friends, I have connected the dots between my past and my present. I have realized that the coping mechanisms that got me through my childhood does not serve who I am today, and I recognise certain thoughts, actions, reactions, and decisions that are born from 'triggers' and 'flashbacks' from a past that I have not completely healed from yet.

Now I can see where my need for a rescuer/saviour as a child always drew me into the same kind of abusive/broken people in relationships, because that is all I ever knew about love growing up! No-one ever taught me how to love or be loved. No-one ever taught me how to take a compliment without being suspicious of hidden intentions behind it. No-one ever taught me what it felt like to feel 'SAFE' in my own home!

Now, as I recognise myself as a child of God, I can see His work in my life – even when I doubted His very existence! I have found the father I never had! I have found what it feels like to be loved unconditionally. He is the one teaching me how to love myself and others through His forgiveness. Through Him, I have found myself … and through Him, I have found the saviour that I have spent my whole life looking for. With him, I am loved, and I am safe!

In the next part of this book – the final chapter, I bare my soul, I stand in my truth, I embrace my faults, and I face my demons! In Him and through Him, I have set myself free from the prison of my own mind. Through song and poetry, I sing God's praise and I give Him all the glory, for without Him, I wouldn't be here. Without Him, I would still be stuck at the rock-bottom of that black abyss that used to consume me daily.

PART FIVE
BOOK OF SONGS — THE FINAL CHAPTER

Jesus is the butterfly effect in our lives...

THE DOMINO EFFECT VS THE BUTTERFLY EFFECT

The blackness that overwhelms our minds VS His strength that empowers our hearts.
The helplessness deep within our souls VS His hope that lightens our hearts.
The heaviness that breaks our physical bodies VS His love that mends our broken hearts.

The Domino Effect:
The violence seeps into our hearts as we become what we hate the most.
The violence in our hearts blackens our souls and throws shade over our minds.
The violence of our past becomes our crutch as we stumble towards our future.
That violence becomes part of who we are as we struggle to become who we yearn to be.

The Butterfly Effect:
HE is the cure to the domino effect of the storms within us that injects itself into our hearts.
HE sheds light into our darkness. HE replaces that violence in our hearts
with His eternal love. HE is the localised change within us which can
lead to a large-scale ripple-effect impact in the world around us.

By changing our hearts amidst the domino effects in our lives, we then change
the world of those around us – isn't that amazing!!!! How can we not sing
with delight about this and give God glory for this miracle of works that hap-
pens within us and around us every single day – if only we let it!

I AM WHO I AM

Coping mechanisms of yesterday won't serve me today
Because disassociation and fear won't let others near
This violence in my heart is tearing my soul apart
And this fight or flight mentality has become my normality

Chorus
Aggression, Repression, Regression
Self-harm, funny farm, sound the alarm
Memory triggers that make me wanna pull the trigger
Grieving a stolen childhood amidst this adult falsehood

There's no-where left to run from things that can't be undone
And there's no way to control the emotions that swallow me whole
There's no shame in the tears that represent my fears
But there's no freedom in the walls that were built amidst my pitfalls

Chorus
Aggression, Repression, Regression
Self-harm, funny farm, sound the alarm
Memory triggers that make me wanna pull the trigger
Grieving a stolen childhood amidst this adult falsehood

Bridge
It doesn't make sense and it's not fair
…but this is no longer my cross to bear
I submit this pain and anger at His feet
…and I cry out His name as I retreat

I am who I am because of where I've been
I am who I am because of what I've seen
I am who I am because of His strength in me
I am who I am because of His power in me

HALLELUJAH! PRAISE THE LORD! THANK YOU JESUS!
Because of you … I am enough
Because of you … I am worthy
Because of you … I am strong
Because of you … I am loved

Repeat last verse – LOUDER!

I WON

I ran from you just as much as I ran from me
I fought against you just as much as I fought against me
Running from what…? Fighting for what…? I could never see
That the truth was in You all along, and also in me
I had won the war already – I was already free

Chorus
Wild by nature but soft at heart
Caged by love – soul torn apart
Looking for love but fighting to be free
A fight to the death – A fight to be me
I won *because in Him I am loved*
I won *because in Him I am free*
I won *because in Him I am free to be me*

Even though I ran from you
Even though I hid from you
Even though I turned my heart against you
You still loved me
You still saved me
You still walked beside me
THAT is your amazing grace!

No more running
No more hiding
No more self-sabotage amidst the devil's camouflage
Now I stand firm in Your word
I face my fears armed with my faith
And I wear Your armour to ward off the works of the snake-charmer

Chorus
Wild by nature but soft at heart
Caged by love – soul torn apart
Looking for love but fighting to be free
A fight to the death – A fight to be me
I won *because in Him I am loved*
I won *because in Him I am free*
I won *because in Him I am free to be me*

WE'RE COVERED

Every day is a battle
Even though we've already won the war
The daily fight against our flesh
Our sinful nature of always wanting more
Nothing we do can save us
A life of good deeds will not save our soul
The paradox of our faith
Is that we win by letting go of control

Chorus
Not my timing Lord, but Yours
Because I am Your vessel in this cause
Not my glory Lord, but Yours
Because I am Your vessel for this cause

In this battle we fight daily
I know we do not fight it alone
Because He started fighting with us
The day they rolled away that stone
Fighting with faith and trust in His word
Gives us leverage in the battles we face
As we shield ourselves with God's armour
We also bask in the light of his grace

Chorus
Not my timing Lord, but Yours
Because I am Your vessel in this cause
Not my glory Lord, but Yours
Because I am Your vessel for this cause

Bridge
Remember that Jesus has won the war for us
Because He laid Himself on the cross for our sin
Remember that He laid Himself bare for **their** sin too
Because He covered us all in that sacrificial win
His love and forgiveness is there for us all - He doesn't set anyone apart
It is His humble act of faith in us that shall create transformation in our heart

IF ONLY

If only I had some warning … if only I knew …
That the monsters under my bed
Were nothing compared to the monsters in my head

If only I had some guidance … if only I knew …
That the demons of my past
Were the shadows that created this outcast

Chorus
We are the hope in hopeless
We are the love in loveless
We are the faith in faithless
We are a positive trapped in a negative
Forever dreaming of what could be … if only …

If only I had something unconditional … if only I knew …
That the waterfalls I've been chasing
Were just distractions from the demons I wasn't facing

If only I had opened my heart … if only I knew …
That the love and peace I was trying to pursue
Was there all along in the everlasting You

Chorus
We are the hope in hopeless
We are the love in loveless
We are the faith in faithless
We are a positive trapped in a negative
Forever dreaming of what could be … if only …

Bridge
Today I stand strong in Your word … today I know …
That there is love and strength in this sickly pod
Because in Your name and Your grace – I am a child of God

Repeat bridge – LOUDER!

COME WHAT MAY

To be like water…
And like a lamb to the slaughter…
Seeing danger in my path…
But staying on task!
Not changing direction…
Not fearing my reflection…
Just flowing…
Just growing…
And just knowing that as a child of God…
My faith in Him will keep me going!

Chorus
Because even when I'm weak or things go wrong,
I will still praise You in heartfelt song!
I know that in You I am strong,
And in Your love is where I belong!

Come what may…
With strength I'll pray…
For His truth against deceit…
And for His lamp at my feet!
For His lighthouse to guide me through life's murky waters,
For his love to reach ALL his sons and daughters!

Chorus
Because even when I'm weak or things go wrong,
I will still praise You in heartfelt song!
I know that in You I am strong,
And in Your love is where I belong!

Because even when WE are weak or things go wrong,
WE will still praise You in heartfelt song!
WE know that in You WE are strong,
And in Your love is where WE belong!

TO YOU GOD WE SHALL TURN

How could I feel what was real when I was stuck in the spiel of my vicious cycle ordeal?
How could I deal with the surreal when Your truth was concealed by my ideals?
How could I heal what had congealed when I couldn't
kneel in appeal for you to take the wheel?
How could I stand in Your truth when I was living a lie???

Bridge
When the love of another is used to smother out the fire in our heart…
To you God we shall turn!
When the promise of forever keeps us tethered to a love that tears our soul apart…
To you God we shall turn!
When the fear of losing control swallows us whole, and the memories of
what they stole kills our soul…one murderous stab at a time…
To you God we shall turn!

Chorus
Because IN you – the truth in my heart has set me free…
Because THROUGH you – the realities in my world I can finally see…
Because FROM you – I learnt who I truly was inside…
And BECAUSE of you – those lies inside have finally died!

No longer living to please…
I stand strong in the breeze of the winds of change.
No longer living in fight, flight, or freeze…
I stand tall amidst the enemies in my head and the frenemies in my world.
No longer looking to appease…
I fall to my knees in surrender and smile…instantly at ease.
I will never be the same again!!!

Chorus
Because IN you – the truth in my heart has set me free…
Because THROUGH you – the realities in my world I can finally see…
Because FROM you – I learnt who I truly was inside…
And BECAUSE of you – those lies inside have finally died!

Thank you Jesus … For yesterday, today, and tomorrow.
Thank you Jesus … For removing all my sorrow.
Thank you Jesus … For releasing me from my past.
Thank you Jesus … For giving me a love that will forever last!

CHILD OF GOD

I will not negotiate or compromise with the lies and disguise of someone else's heart.
I will not relax while my heart reacts and counteracts to the lack of kindness around me.
I will not be hung by their tongue and hide the unsung hero of my life anymore!

Chorus
I shall rise in His power...
I shall stand in His strength ...
I shall speak His truth with pride ...
And I shall sing his glory with fervour ... today, tomorrow, and forever!

When I lost all my hope – I found Gods help ...
When I lost all my possessions – God restored my health ...
When I lost sight of the truth – I found God's word in my mouth ...
When I lost everything around me – I found myself ...
... IN HIM
... THROUGH HIM
... BECAUSE OF HIM!

Chorus
I shall rise in His power...
I shall stand in His strength ...
I shall speak His truth with pride ...
And I shall sing his glory with fervour ... today, tomorrow, and forever!

Bridge
As a child of God ... I am His humble servant ...
As a child of God ... I am an enemy of the serpent ...
As a child of God ... I am His soldier in this spiritual war ...
As a child of God ... I shall fight in His name forever more!

Chorus
I shall rise in His power...
I shall stand in His strength ...
I shall speak His truth with pride ...
And I shall sing his glory with fervour ... today, tomorrow, and forever!

THANK YOU JESUS

A face for those who feel faceless …
A name for those who feel nameless …
A voice for those who feel voiceless …
A home for those who feel homeless …

__Chorus__
I am His child …
I am His friend …
I am His servant!
His love surrounds me …
His grace comforts me …
His mercy frees me!

His face against our adversary …
His shield against their controversy …
His name against our adversity …
His word against their perversity …

__Chorus__
I am His child …
I am His friend …
I am His servant!
His love surrounds me …
His grace comforts me …
His mercy frees me!

__Bridge__
JEEEEEEESUS!!!
He is our refuge!
No-one shall He refuse!
His grace and mercy cover us all!
His love and strength shields us all!

THAAAAANK YOOOOOU JEEEEESUS
THAAAAANK YOOOOOU JEEEEESUS
THAAAAANK YOOOOOU JEEEEESUS
THAAAAANK YOOOOOU JEEEEESUS

I AM HIS - HE IS MINE

With His truth in my heart, and my heart on my sleeve …
I know I'll never be alone because I know He'll never leave.

I am His – He is mine!
Forever loved – a gift divine!
His armour protects me!
His word affirms me!
His love empowers me!
His grace frees me!

With His lamp at my feet, and His light on my path …
I know He's in my future – despite my unruly past.

I am His – He is mine!
Forever loved – a gift divine!
His armour protects me!
His word affirms me!
His love empowers me!
His grace frees me!

With His peace in my mind, and the joy on my face …
I know I'm not perfect – but I am saved by His grace!

I am His – He is mine!
Forever loved – a gift divine!
His armour protects me!
His word affirms me!
His love empowers me!
His grace frees me!

HALLELUJAH – THANK YOU JESUS
HALLELUJAH – THANK YOU JESUS
I LOVE YOU!

WHISPERS OF THE HEART

Maori followed by English translation

Kaua e korero toku tamahine.
Whakarongo mai.

He aha ahau whakarongo i ki?

Ki toku reo …
Ki toku wairua …
Ki toku Rangimarie mo koutou.
Kia noho tonu …. Sssshhhhh …

I am with you …
I am in you …
You are not alone!

TRANSLATION:

Don't talk my daughter.
Listen to me.

What am I listening to?

My voice …
My spirit …
My peace for you.
Be still … sssshhhhh …

I am with you …
I am in you …
You are not alone!

Suspicious eyes tells us lies, taints the heart and tears love apart!

To truly appreciate the light in my life, you must first understand the darkness that used to consume me. Journey with me through these pages of real life, real struggles, real hope and real salvation!

May my words speak into the hearts of those who
feel hopeless, voiceless and/or powerless.
May my truth lead you to Gods' truth, and may we ALL feel
empowered by His love, His strength and His grace.
You are not alone.

www.ingramcontent.com/pod-product-compliance
Lightning Source LLC
Chambersburg PA
CBHW060146050426
42448CB00010B/2319